Asset Protection &Retirement
in New Hampshire:
Avoiding Financial Disaster
Caused By A Nursing Home Stay

**A Legal and Financial Guide
to Surviving the Asset-Draining
Effects of a Long-Term Nursing
Home Stay**

Edward D. Beasley, JD, LLM
David H. Ferber, JD
Gregory B. Gagne, ChFC

Library of Congress Control No: 2005908221
ISBN 0-9772745-0-0

Printed in the United States of America by Mennonite Press, Inc., Newton, Kansas.

Book Design by Larry G. Nichols II

Published by Beasley & Ferber, PA, Concord New Hampshire, and Affinity Investment Group, LLC, Exeter, New Hampshire.

For additional copies, send $24.95 plus $3.00 shipping and handling per book to:

Beasley & Ferber, PA	or	Affinity Investment Group, LLC
55 Hall Street		12 String Bridge
Concord, NH 03301		Exeter, NH 03833
(603) 225-5010		(603) 778-6436

Dedication

We dedicate this book to the great many clients and friends who took the time to communicate with their legislators and the governor against Medicaid cutbacks. We have no doubt that their efforts led to the government scaling back the harshest elements of Granite Care. We owe the clients and friends our gratitude, and they should be proud of themselves.

Edward D. Beasley
David H. Ferber

People like my mother and father and my mother- and father-in-law have worked a lifetime to obtain the American dream of achieving financial independence, enjoying the "good life." It is to those who have taught me life's valuable lessons of how to succeed while doing the right things that I dedicate this book

Gregory B. Gagne

Table of Contents

PART TWO: FINANCIAL AND ESTATE PLANNING
                     FOR RETIREMENT ACCOUNTS

About the Authors:

Edward D. Beasley, JD, LLM: Attorney Beasley is the founder of Beasley & Ferber, P.A., an estate planning and elder law firm with offices in Concord, Bedford, Nashua and Portsmouth, New Hampshire and North Andover, Massachusetts. He received his Bachelor's Degree, Summa Cum Laude, Phi Beta Kappa, from Dartmouth College (1974), his Juris Doctor Degree, Cum Laude, from Washington & Lee University (1978) and his LLM Degree in Taxation from Boston University (1982).

Mr. Beasley has written and published numerous articles on estate planning and elder law, including "Trusts For the Average Person," "The Nursing Home Crunch," and "The Ethics of Medicaid Planning." He has appeared as a featured guest on NBC's National Nightly News with Tom Brokaw in a segment entitled "Inheritance Disputes." Attorney Beasley was also featured in a USA TODAY cover story entitled "Fighting Over the Care of Aging Parents." He is co-author of the books, "Alzheimer's Disease: Fighting for Financial Survival" and "The Nursing Home Crunch." He lectures frequently on the topic of Elder Law and the legal steps available to protect the life savings of a loved one afflicted with Alzheimer's Disease. He has been a guest on New Hampshire Public Radio, speaking about nursing home planning.

Mr. Beasley is former Chair of the Elder Law Committee of the American Bar Association (General Practice, Solo and Small Firm Section). He is also a member of the National Academy of Elder Law Attorneys. Mr. Beasley is recognized nationally as an expert in the fields of elder law, Medicaid and nursing home planning, and asset preservation techniques for those afflicted with dementia in general and the dementing illnesses known as Alzheimer's disease, Huntington's disease and Lou Gehrig's disease (ALS – amyothrophic lateral sclerosis) in particular.

David H. Ferber, JD: Attorney Ferber is a partner with Beasley & Ferber, P.A. He received his Bachelor's Degree in Psychology, Magna Cum Laude, Phi Beta Kappa, from Columbia University (1981) and his Juris Doctor Degree from Columbia University Law School (1984), where he was a member of the Columbia Human Rights Law Review.

Mr. Ferber is a nationally-published author of articles on estate and Medicaid planning, including articles on charitable remainder trusts, the use of annuities in Medicaid planning, the use of disclaimers in estate planning, qualified personal residence trusts and the joint revocable trust as a tool for estate and Medicaid planning, among others. He is also the author of articles on estate planning for the Concord Monitor, Concord, N.H., and the Laconia Citizen, Laconia, N.H. He is co-author of the books, "Alzheimer's Disease: Fighting for Financial Survival" and "The Nursing Home Crunch." He is a frequent lecturer on estate and Medicaid planning, having given presentations on estate planning for the State of New Hampshire Division of

Elderly and Adult Services, for other attorneys, social workers and for the general public. He has been a guest on WMUR-TV, speaking about nursing home planning.

Mr. Ferber is former Vice Chair and Newsletter Editor of the Elder Law Committee of the American Bar Association (General Practice, Solo and Small Firm Section) and is a member of the National Academy of Elder Law Attorneys. He is on the board of directors of the New Hampshire Family Support Partnerships, and is a former board member of the New Hampshire Coalition Against Elder Abuse, a former commissioner of the Laconia, New Hampshire, Conservation Commission and a former board member of the Stamford, Connecticut, Shelter for the Homeless. He is a member of the bars of New Hampshire, Massachusetts, Maine and Connecticut.

Gregory B. Gagne, ChFC: Mr. Gagne is the founder of Affinity Investment Group, LLC, an investment advisory firm registered with the United States Securities and Exchange Commission. His firm offers wealth management and distribution planning services for retirees or those planning to retire.

After earning his Bachelor of Science, a dual degree in economics and finance, from Bentley College in 1992, Greg became a Chartered Financial Consultant in 2001 following completion of courses in estate planning, financial planning, business planning, income tax, and retirement and pension planning through the American College.

A member of the New Hampshire Chapter of the Society of Financial Service Professionals, Greg is also past president of the New Hampshire Association of Insurance and

Financial Advisors, having served previously in many chairs of its local board. He is a member of the Financial Planning Association.

Greg has garnered national exposure in professional trade magazine articles on practice management and planning issues and is also a sought-after speaker on these subjects.

Greg has been awarded the National Quality Award (NQA) for persistence and quality of business and is also a repeat qualifier for the Million Dollar Round Table (MDRT), which represents the top 10% of financial service professionals worldwide.

Foreword

"Many of life's failures are by people who did not realize how close they were to success when they gave up."

—*Thomas A Edison*

Our forefathers had the foresight to envision the wonderful opportunities our country could provide for the average person. Their foundation laid a path for hard-working Americans to follow and then eventually create new paths of prosperity in our land.

Hard-working men and women spent their lives in the nearby mill buildings creating their own version of the "American Dream." The problem then and today is that so many folks are focused on their work that they never take the time to properly plan for the day when they may no longer be active in the workforce.

The purpose of this book is to teach you how to prepare for that event or, if already retired, to put in place the proper foundation to protect the nest egg that you have spent a lifetime creating.

This book is intended to be an easily understood guide for the average person. You need not be a legal or an investment expert to understand the concepts and "blueprints" of the time-tested and proven methods to creating a lasting financial and estate plan for you and your family.

Most retirees grew up at the end of the Depression or shortly thereafter. The valuable lessons from that time have been ingrained into many seniors' psyches. Many seniors have done without, saved considerable sums of money, and built a substantial net worth. It is time to take the next step and protect what you have created.

Chapter 1:

What is a Prosperous Retirement?

"If parents pass enthusiasm along to their children, they will leave them an estate of incalculable value."

—*Thomas A Edison*

This question is not easily answered. There are many correct answers, including health, happiness, and significant financial assets. When all the various answers are boiled down they equate to time freedom and financial freedom; the ability to do what you want when you want and how you want.

Our firms have had the opportunity to interview thousands of families in the Northeast to ask this very question: what is a prosperous retirement? We have learned a great deal over the last several years from these interviews and are honored to share the results with you.

For most folks it is the ability to afford the "wants" and not just the "needs" of life and the capacity to enjoy sharing with their families and community. There are hundreds if not thousands of books available that explain how to create the best portfolio, pick the best stock, seek the highest interest rate, outwit the stock market, but we have yet to find a quality book to speak to the heart of the retiree. Yes, we want to increase our net worth, but what about achieving and maintaining a balance during the "golden" years?

The issues of the utmost importance to the people ous firms have interviewed over the past several years include:

Health
Happiness
Preservation of capital
Protection of assets in the event of a nursing
    home stay
Assisting the grandchildren in obtaining higher
    education
Philanthropic intentions
Instilling values into the younger generations
Taking the "trip of a lifetime"
Protecting their spouse
Leaving a legacy for children

It takes a sound business plan for your finances to achieve these various goals. We will spend the remainder of this book reviewing the building blocks you should utilize to fulfill your goals and objectives and to create a legacy for you and your family. Learn the valuable lessons from others' mistakes so that you will not have to repeat them.

Chapter 2:

Basic Estate Planning: Wills, Trusts, and Powers of Attorney in New Hampshire

A. Wills

Every adult, regardless of age and level of assets, should have a solid estate plan. Doing an estate plan will ensure that your assets will pass to the people you want and will also protect you and your family in the event you become incapacitated or disabled. An estate plan can be designed to minimize taxes, probate fees and administration costs and, most important, give you piece of mind about your family's security. There are five documents that typically go into an estate plan: a trust, will, durable power of attorney, medical power of attorney and living will declaration.

A will, as most people know, is a legal document that passes assets to the heirs on death.[1] A surprising number of people think that a will avoids probate; however,

---

[1]Technically, an "heir" is someone who will inherit your estate through the laws of intestate succession if you do not have a will. In this book, when we use the word "heirs," we will use it in the non-technical sense, as being synonymous with "beneficiaries."

exactly the opposite is true, in that wills are subject to the probate process. When someone dies in New Hampshire, his or her will is filed with the probate court for the county in which the person lived, along with a petition for appointment of an executor. (Most people think that the person you name as executor automatically becomes executor on your death. In fact, the court has to formally appoint the executor before he can act.) When the will and petition for probate administration are filed, here is what the court does:

1. *Determines whether the will is valid.*

In order to be valid, the will must be prepared strictly in accordance with certain formalities. To be valid, a will needs to have been signed by the decedent in the presence of two witnesses. All three persons (decedent and witnesses) need to have signed in the presence of each other and in the presence of a notary public or justice of the peace. The witnesses cannot be interested parties to the will (*i.e.*, they cannot be beneficiaries or otherwise named in the will). The notary or justice of the peace needs to have signed a formal affidavit attesting to the manner of execution. If such an affidavit, known as a "self-proving affidavit," has not been signed, then one of the witnesses will need to testify in court as to the manner of execution of the will. If the will was prepared in another state, an affidavit from an attorney in that state must be filed stating that the will was properly prepared in accordance with that state's laws. Most probate courts in the state handle the above procedures through the mail, but it is always in the discretion of the judge to have the proposed executor or attorney come to court personally.

There are two interesting facts about wills in New Hampshire that most people do not know. First, if the decedent wrote the will and later got divorced, then the divorce will automatically make void any provision in the will for the ex-spouse, including a provision naming such spouse as executor. Second, if the decedent has a deceased child who is not named in the will, and if that deceased child has children, those children will be entitled to a share of the estate.

2. *Sets the amount of the bond.*

Even though most wills state that the executor is to serve without bond, or with a minimum bond, the courts do not honor such directions. A probate bond is a type of insurance contract. For a fee, the insurance company will make good any losses caused by the executor's dishonesty or theft of funds. If the executor misappropriates funds and the insurance company reimburses the estate, the company will then have a claim against the executor. The court will set the bond proportionately to the executor's estimate of assets in the estate. Once the bond has been set, though, the court will typically agree to lower the amount of the bond, if all of the beneficiaries consent. This is a cost-saving measure, since the higher the amount of the bond, the more it costs. The bond premium is paid annually, and the bond must be renewed if the probate proceeding extends more than one year.

3. *Appoints the executor.*

After the will has been accepted by the court and the bond has been purchased, then the court formally appoints the executor by issuing a "Certificate of Appointment." This is a document with the court seal.

The first legal duty of the executor is to give a formal notice to all persons mentioned in the will, certain other relatives specified by law, and known creditors of the deceased. The executor then makes an inventory of all of the assets to be probated and reports that inventory, under oath, to the court. The inventory stays on file with the court and is a matter of public record. Next, the executor collects the assets and paysthe decedent's final expenses, debts and taxes. Creditors have six months to file any claims against the estate and one year to file any lawsuits against the estate. If there are any estate taxes, the executor, before closing the estate, needs to obtain a release, *i.e.*, a document stating that all taxes are paid, from the state taxing authorities. At the end of the probate proceedings, before the assets can be distributed to the beneficiaries, the executor makes a report to the judge of all that he has done, as well as a report of the income and expenditures of the estate. This report is known as an "accounting."It is only after the judge approves of the accounting that the assets can be distributed to the heirs.

Recently, New Hampshire adopted a procedure whereby as long as all of the decedent's bills have been paid and all of the beneficiaries have consented, the executor can close the estate without an accounting. This procedure is known as "Summary Administration." The state has also simplified the probate procedure in the case of husband

and wife and situations in which the will names only one beneficiary. If there is a surviving spouse (or if the spouse has died and there is an only child) and if this person is sole beneficiary and named executor, then he or she can request a "Waiver of Administration." With Waiver of Administration, most of the formal requirements of probate are not required, and the process is fairly simple. Finally, small estates under $10,000 are eligible for "Voluntary Administration," which is a streamlined and faster version of full probate administration.

B. *Trusts*

Someone who wants to avoid the probate process for his family can prepare a trust instead of a traditional will. The revocable trust, also known as a living trust, is a substitute for a traditional will. In large part, the trust says the same thing as a will, *i.e.*, who is going to inherit the assets and who the trustee (the functional equivalent of an executor) is to be. The crucial difference between a trust and a will, however, is that the will is subject to probate upon death, whereas the trust is not.

A trust has three parties, the "grantor," who is the person who sets up the trust, the "trustee," who is the person who manages the trust, and the "beneficiary," who is the person who will get the benefit from the trust or who will inherit the assets. When you set up a living trust, you wear all three hats, in that you are the grantor, trustee and beneficiary. You place your assets in the name of the trust, and then go about your business exactly as usual. When you die, or if you become incompetent, a successor trustee of your choice, usually one or two of your children, takes over management of the trust. Ultimately, at your death, the beneficiaries you have named in the trust will inherit the trust assets without probate. In almost all cases, there are no legal fees to settle the trust, and settlement of your estate proceeds quickly and privately. The formalities and procedures described above for probate do not occur. Years ago, it was mainly the wealthy that did trusts, while most other people did wills. These days, living trusts have become standard estate planning tools for people of moderate means, not only just the wealthy.

In 2004, New Hampshire adopted a law known as the "Uniform Trust Code." A "uniform" law is written with the expectation that it will be adopted by most states, and will therefore be identical (hence the term uniform) throughout most or all of the country. There are a number of uniform laws that pertain to estate planning, such as the Uniform Transfers to Minors Act, Uniform Simultaneous Death Act, Uniform Testamentary Additions to Trust Act and Uniform Probate Code. As people become more and more mobile, and often retire to the Sunbelt or the West, it becomes more important that a trust you did in New Hampshire be interpreted and administered in your new state the same way as in your old. Similarly, these days most people's children live in different states throughout the country, so it is important that their rights under the trust be the same regardless of where they live. The Uniform Trust Code helps to achieve these goals.

For the most part, the Uniform Trust Code only applies to irrevocable trusts (discussed later in the book) and not to revocable living trusts. However, it is important to understand that if you have a trust and later pass away or become incompetent, your trust will become irrevocable. In that case, the Uniform Trust Code will apply to the trust. The Code is about 40 pages long, and a full explanation is way beyond the scope of this book. For our purposes, the most important part of the Uniform Trust Code is those provisions concerning notice to the beneficiaries. Within 60 days of a revocable trust having become irrevocable due to death or incompetency, the successor trustee (usually one of the children) needs to notify the beneficiaries that the trust exists, and that they have a right to a copy of the trust, as well as periodic reports of the trust assets. Such notification is a good idea, since otherwise the beneficiaries might not even know that the trust exists. It is also possible for the beneficiaries to waive their rights to these notices, and many beneficiaries do so as a way of honoring their parents' request that the trust be kept confidential until their deaths.

Whether you opt for a will or a living trust in your estate plan, special care must be taken if one of the spouses is ill or might need nursing home care. Most wills and trusts for married couples naturally leave all of the assets to the surviving spouse. If one of the spouses is a permanent resident of a nursing home, however, care must be taken to avoid automatically naming that spouse as beneficiary. Let's say that one spouse is in the nursing home and is receiving Medicaid benefits. The couple has a will or trust that leaves everything to the survivor. If the healthy spouse unexpectedly dies first, then all of the assets will go to the nursing home spouse. He or she will immediately lose

Medicaid coverage and will have to spend down the inheritance. It is likely that the children will receive nothing. To avoid this situation, the couple could have amended their estate planning documents to say that if the healthy spouse dies first, the assets would pass to the children instead of the sick spouse. They should also amend the beneficiary designations on their life insurance and IRAs in the same way.

C. *Durable Financial Powers of Attorney*

Someone who has become mentally (and sometimes physically) incompetent does not have the legal capacity to transact business, such as paying bills, signing tax returns, buying or selling property or making contracts. When an incompetent person has not done adequate estate planning, someone such as a spouse, adult child or other interested party must petition the probate court to become guardian over the estate. The court-appointed guardian can then transact business as representative for the incompetent person.

To obtain guardianship in New Hampshire, you have to prove to the court's satisfaction that the person cannot take care of his or her financial or business affairs. The court will hold a hearing, and you will have to present specific testimony and evidence to convince the judge that the person is in need of help. If you prove this, the court will grant you only the specific authority you need and no more. The benefits of guardianship are that the court oversees what the guardian does, and the guardian must be bonded. On the other hand, guardianship can be time-consuming, expensive and cumbersome. The attorneys must be paid, you need to testify in court and buy a bond, and you must make periodic reports to the court as to all financial transactions. There is a law in New Hampshire that allows you to name your guardian in advance, should the necessity for one arise, and to specify whom you would *not* like to be guardian. Even if you structure your affairs to avoid guardianship, as discussed below, it would be a good idea to sign such a document, just to be on the safe side.

Those who are interested in protecting their assets from long-term care might want to structure their affairs so that they never need a guardian, as guardianship in New Hampshire can completely destroy your ability to shelter assets. That is, in order to be able to implement any of the asset protection strategies described in later chapters of this book, the guardian must get the court's permission. Although there is a statute by which the court can authorize the guardian to preserve assets, it is unlikely that the court would ever do so; that is, the role of the probate judge is to "preserve" the assets for use by the incapacitated person, even if such "preservation" means depletion by payments to the nursing home. In our experience, most people would want to save their assets for use by their spouse and would want to leave their children a modest inheritance, but seeing to these obvious, common-sense intentions is not the role of the probate court. The court's role is to see to it that the person's assets are used for his or her care, even if the spouse is impoverished and the inheritance is lost, and that Medicaid is used as a last resort.

In order to avoid guardianship proceedings, your estate plan can put in place a document known as a "Durable Power of Attorney (DPOA)." If you become incompetent, the holder of your DPOA (called the "Attorney in Fact" or agent) can transact your business for you, much as a guardian would do, but without reporting to the probate court. If you insert Medicaid planning provisions in the DPOA (discussed in later chapters), then the attorney-in-fact would be able to act to shelter assets for you. DPOAs in New Hampshire have traditionally been informal documents, but in recent years the legislature has put in place an increasing number of requirements and protections, described here:

1. *Disclosure statement.*

Every DPOA in New Hampshire must have attached two disclosure statements, one signed by the principal and one signed by the agent.   The principal's statement is a reminder to him or her that the agent has broad powers and essentially is a warning that the principal needs to have the utmost faith and confidence in the person he appoints as agent.   The agent needs to sign a statement which explains that he owes the highest duties of care, faith and loyalty to the principal and that he must at all times act in the best interests of the principal.

2. *Gifting by the agent.*

Recently, the state legislature has imposed significant limits on the right of the principal to make gifts of the agent's assets. A 2004 law says that in order for an agent to make gifts using a durable power of attorney, the power of attorney must contain specific authority for the agent to do so. The statute says:

V   (a) An attorney in fact is not authorized to make gifts, pursuant to the durable power of attorney, to the attorney in fact or to others unless:

    (1) The durable power of attorney explicitly authorizes gifts; and

    (2) The proposed gift will not leave the principal without sufficient assets or income to provide for the principal's care without relying on Medicaid, other public assistance or charity, unless the authority to make such a gift is expressly conferred, or the gift is approved in advance by the court upon a determination that the gift is authorized in accordance with RSA 506:7, III(e).

    (b) No attorney in fact may make a gift to himself or herself of property belonging to the principal unless the terms of the power of attorney explicitly provide for the authority to make gifts to the attorney in fact, or the gift is approved in advance by the court upon a determination that the gift is authorized in accordance with RSA 506:7, III(e).

NH RSA 506:6(V)

It is evident from the statute that the legislature tried to address the perceived problem that agents under DPOAs were making gifts without adequately considering the Medicaid implications.

D. *Advance Directives: Living Wills and Medical Powers of Attorney*

It is very important for an estate plan to include a medical power of attorney and a living will. Also known as "Advance Directives," these documents deal with medical and end-of-life decisions. Essentially, the medical power of attorney allows your spouse, children or other trusted person you name to make medical decisions for you if you are unable to do so.

If you become incompetent and do not have a medical power of attorney, your family would need to seek a court guardianship. Clearly, signing the medical power of attorney will avoid lengthy and potentially costly court proceedings in time of crisis. In New Hampshire, as in all states, the medical power of attorney is a standard form. It is available at any hospital and many senior's centers.

An interesting issue that has arisen in recent years is the interplay of the medical power of attorney and the federal medical privacy laws, or "HIPPA" laws. The HIPPA laws strictly regulate medical privacy issues. While a discussion of those laws is beyond the scope of this book, suffice it to say that it is far from clear as to whether those laws permit medical personnel to discuss your case with the health care power of attorney. To solve this problem, health care powers of attorney should contain HIPPA provisions which allow disclosure of these issues to your power of attorney. As of yet, the health care power of attorney statute has not been amended to make the form "HIPPA compliant," but it is the practice of the authors to add HIPPA provisions to the health care powers of attorney that we prepare.

When someone signs a health care power of attorney, it is customary to sign a living will at the same time. The living will is the document that directs the removal of life-sustaining treatment in a situation where you are terminally ill with no hope of recovery. Recently, the heart-wrenching case-of Terry Schiavo drove home to the entire country the importance of having a living will and the tragic consequences of not having one. Avoid the temptation to use a form from a magazine or computer program, as New Hampshire has a specific form of living will that is recognized by law.

Chapter 3:

The Medicaid Rules

A. The Difference Between Medicare and Medicaid

Medicare is the basic health insurance program available to anyone who is disabled or over 65 and has paid into the Social Security system. Many people believe that Medicare pays for long-term nursing home care. However, people who believe this and who later enter a nursing home are in for a very unpleasant and expensive surprise, since Medicare is **not** designed to cover long-term nursing home care. If a Medicare beneficiary spends three nights in the hospital and then goes to a nursing home for rehabilitation, Medicare will pay the nursing home in full for the first 20 days and then in part from day 21 to 100. However, once the patient stops making improvement, Medicare and the Medicare supplement stop paying, even if this occurs before expiration of the hundred days. Thus, Medicare for skilled nursing care is meant to be a short-term benefit only. People who need long-term nursing home care are not covered.

B. *Three Ways of Paying for Nursing Homes*

Since Medicare will not cover long-term care, what will? There are three ways to pay for a nursing home: long-term care insurance, private payment, and Medicaid.[1]

1. *Long-Term Care Insurance*

Long-term care insurance is a type of health insurance that will pay for prolonged nursing home stays provided that the conditions of the insurance policy are met. Depending on the policy, payment can be for as little as two years, or for as long as a lifetime. The insurance can pay anywhere from a minimal amount of the nursing home charge, all the way to payment in full. The better policies come with an "inflation rider," which means that the policy benefit rises each year. Some policies also include payment for home health care.

Since nursing home insurance decreases people's reliance on Medicaid, the government is enacting policies that encourage people to buy this insurance. Under federal law, the premiums for certain long-term care policies are deductible in part as a medical expense. New Hampshire has recently enacted a law, part of the Granite Care Medicaid Modernization Plan, which states that holders of certain long-term care policies will be exempt from the Medicaid spend-down and estate recovery rules; i.e., the

---

[1] According to the Federal Centers for Medicare & Medicaid Services, for the years 1980 to 2003, Medicaid paid 46.0% of nursing home costs, private funds paid for 27.9%, Medicare paid for 12.4%, private insurance paid for 7.7% and other sources paid 6.1%. See Centers for Medicare and Medicaid Services, Nat'l. Health Expenditures by Type of Service and Source of Funds, Calendar Years 1980-03, *quoted in* E. O'Brien, "Medicaid's Coverage of Nursing Home Costs: Asset Shelter for the Wealthy or Essential Safety Net," Georgetown University, May 2005, p. 1.

holder of such a policy will not have to spend down his assets on nursing home care, and the state will not put a claim against those assets once the person dies. In order to qualify for these benefits, the insurance policy must:

1. Pay benefits for at least three years, and
2. Have an inflation rider of at least 5% per year, and
3. Have a benefit that pays for at least as much as the average charge for county nursing homes.

This law is not effective yet but will only become effective if the federal government grants the state what is known as a Medicaid Waiver. (Medicaid waivers are discussed in more detail later on.) Whether or when the federal government will grant such a waiver is unknown.

Unfortunately, long-term care insurance is not a one-size-fits-all solution, for two reasons. First, it is simply too expensive for many senior citizens to afford, especially in this age of low interest rates and rising medical costs and gasoline and heating prices. Second, not everyone qualifies for the insurance. The insurance companies set standards as to whom they will insure, and, depending on a person's health, he might not meet the company's standards. For these reasons, one of the criticisms of this segment of Granite Care is that the long-term care exception favors the younger and more affluent – who can qualify for and afford the insurance – and discriminates against the older and less affluent. Simply put, under the state's proposed plan, if you can afford the insurance and can get it, you will be able to protect your assets, and if you can't afford or can't get the insurance, you will lose your assets. On its face, this is grossly unfair and snobbish, and is not the traditional New Hampshire way of doing things. However, given these economic times, it is the new reality.

a. *Components of Long-Term Care Insurance*

A long-term care insurance policy will help pay for the costs of the nursing home provided certain policy conditions are met. The policy provisions that will trigger the payments are called Activities of Daily Living or "ADLs." For most major insurance companies, if the policyholder fails two of these ADLs the policy will enter a payout mode.

ADLs include eating, bathing, dressing, using the bathroom, continence, and transferring. Failing the ADLs usually requires the certification from a physician prior to the insurance company making any payments.

There are many decisions that need to be considered when researching a purchase of long-term care insurance. These include:

1. Your Age. The older you are, the more a policy will cost.
2. Daily Benefit Amount. With the average cost of a nursing home stay ranging from $225 to over $300 per day, you will want to pick a daily benefit amount that covers the cost of the average. Keep in mind that not all people will need to cover 100% of the cost if they receive a pension benefit or Social Security.
3. Elimination Period. This is the amount of time required prior to policy beginning to make payments. Most policies have 0-, 90-, 120-, or even 180-day elimination

periods prior to the commencement of the benefits. The most popular choice among brokers and seniors is 90 days due to the "dovetailing" with the Medicare system.

4. Length of Benefit. Most policies will pay for as little as 3 years and as much as a lifetime of benefit. The average stay in a nursing home based on a study conducted in September 2004 by Met Life Mature Market Institute is 2.4 years. This makes the average cost of a nursing home stay of this length based on a daily rate of $225 approximately $198,000.

5. Inflation Protection. The daily rate of a nursing home stay continues to inflate at a rapid rate. One method to protect against the future cost of the nursing home is to add an inflation rider to the policy. The inflation rider is usually either a 5% simple or 5% compounded based on the base benefit you select. Depending on your age and other financial circumstances, this inflation protection is a very important "add-on" to a long term care policy.

Problems

There are drawbacks to consider when researching the long- term care insurance option.

First, many people simply cannot afford the premiums required to obtain this coverage. Married couples age 65 can expect to pay $6000 to $10,000 per year for coverage depending on the insurance company. For this example, the insurance company will pay for 5 years, provide $200 per day in benefit, and use a 90-day elimination period with 5% compound inflation. For many seniors these premiums are simply out of reach.

The second drawback is that for most companies these premiums are "guaranteed renewable." This means once you have been approved the insurance company can never deny your ability to be covered, but they reserve the right to increase premiums on a "class" basis if approved by the Insurance Department of the state in which they are trying to increase premiums. These rate increases have occurred with some of the largest insurance companies in our country in the last two years, and some insurance carriers have eliminated selling long-term care from their product portfolios altogether.

The third drawback and most common problem with purchasing long-term care insurance is the fact that the insurance companies review your health prior to making an offer to extend coverage. Many seniors simply cannot qualify for the coverage due to health issues.

Advantages

There are several advantages for those who can qualify for long-term care insurance both financially and health-wise.

First, with this coverage you are afforded choice for home health care, choice of nursing home, and financial peace of mind knowing you have dollars that will help cover the cost of a nursing home stay.

Second, there are strategies in this book to help you protect your home, your cottage at the lake, and your stocks, bonds, and cash, but your retirement plans cannot be covered via these techniques and thus will remain as a spend-down asset. The proper placement of long term care insurance will allow you to protect your retirement accounts from the draining effects created by a nursing home stay. This insurance coverage, when appropriately positioned as part of your estate plan, can significantly help you protect your assets for yourself and your family.

Finally, it is important, from a due diligence standpoint, that you take the time to review whether this insurance is feasible in your estate and financial planning situation. The appropriate placement of this coverage will give you choice and time in implementing other planning strategies if a disability strikes.

2. *Private Payment*

Since relatively few people have long-term care insurance, most people who enter the nursing home begin by paying privately. The problem, of course, is that nursing homes are extremely expensive. It is not unusual for a nursing home to cost upwards of $7,000 per month, and very few people can withstand such a payment without quickly exhausting their savings. When the money runs out, nursing home residents are forced to turn to the next method of payment, which is Medicaid.

3. *Medicaid*

Medicaid is a government program that is administered by the states pursuant to federal requirements. It pays for medical treatment and room and board at the nursing home when you have run out of funds. In New Hampshire, the cost of Medicaid is shared by the federal, state and county governments. Currently, nursing home Medicaid is under attack all over the country. Since nursing homes are enormously expensive, it is not unusual for nursing home Medicaid to be among the largest items of most state's budgets. Certainly that is the case in New Hampshire; unfortunately, starting in late 2004 with the Granite Care Plan, New Hampshire has become increasingly aggressive in trying to cut back on nursing home Medicaid eligibility. The ways in which the state has done this are explained throughout this chapter and the rest of the book.

a. *Applying for Medicaid*

In order to qualify for Medicaid, you must meet certain medical and financial requirements. First, you must either live in a nursing home or have a medical need that requires nursing home care. Applications for Medicaid benefits are filed with the Medicaid District Office covering the geographical area in which the applicant lives. After the application is received, the District Office will schedule a personal interview, at which the case technician will go over the documentation that was submitted with the application. Known as "verifications," this documentation is the key to filing a successful Medicaid application. At a minimum, you will have to provide the following verifications:

1. Residence – copy of deed or lease.
2. Age and citizenship – copy of birth or baptismal certificate, naturalization certificate, or green card.
3. Social Security, Medicare and private health insurance cards. If there is private health insurance, then a copy of the latest bill will also be required.

4. Marriage certificate, for married applicants.
5. Current bank account statements, and, frequently, checking statements going back one year, and sometimes three years. You will need to explain and document any large or unusual withdrawals.
6. Statement of nursing home personal needs account.
7. Life insurance policies and statement of cash value for all policies which have a combined face value of $1,500 or more.
8. Copy of durable power of attorney.
9. All trust documents, along with verification of all assets in the trust name.
10. Prepaid burial contract and cemetery deed.
11. Verification of all other financial assets, such as stocks bonds, mutual funds, etc., and the value thereof.
12. Copies of any annuity contracts.
13. Verification of any assets transferred within the past 36 months, or 60 months, in the case of a trust. This requirement applies not only to gifts, but to any asset sold within the relevant time frame. In the case of a house sale, for example, a deed and closing statement will be required.
14. Verification of all income, such as Social Security award statements and pension check stubs. For income that is direct deposited, a bank statement will do.
15. If bank accounts or other assets have been closed in the past three years, an accounting of the proceeds of these accounts.

Providing these verifications can be the most tedious and difficult part the application process. However, it is of the utmost importance, as an application will not be approved until all verifications have been provided, and all issues raised by the verifications have been explained. The burden of providing the verifications is on the applicant; the Medicaid office will not assist you in getting these documents. In recent years, the state has become ever so strict, sometimes to the point of harassment, in enforcing this requirement. One of the authors was once involved in a Medicaid application in which the case technician wanted explanations of routine ATM withdrawals. Further, there are fairly tight time deadlines in providing these verifications, and an application in which the verifications are not provided within the deadlines will be denied. For this reason, it is advisable to assemble the verifications *before* filing the application.

In New Hampshire, while most of the Medicaid case technicians try to be helpful and understanding, the interview and application process is lengthy and frequently can be grueling. Many clients go through the process and later feel as if they have been put on trial. As of this writing, it is not unusual for the state to take four to five months before issuing a Medicaid decision; the state's official policy of processing a completed application within 45 days is routinely ignored. Unfortunately, this situation does not seem to be getting any better. During the time that the application is pending, clients have begun to report that nursing homes have been dunning them for payment.

Under federal law, a Medicaid application can seek payments retroactive to the three months prior to when the application was filed. However, since the application process itself can take two to three months, and sometimes longer, and since the nursing home is not being paid while application is pending, you would be well advised to start the process before running out of money, rather than after. A good rule of thumb is to file the application while you have three months' worth of private funds available.

If you are dissatisfied with the results of the application, you can claim an appeal that is known as a "fair hearing." The fair hearing is not a "second chance." Rather, it is a proceeding at which you will have to prove that the caseworker wrongfully denied the application, due to a mistake of fact or a mistake in applying the law. Fair hearings are conducted by a "hearings examiner," who is an employee of the state or of the Medicaid agency. At a fair hearing, each side will have the ability to offer evidence and state the legal basis of his or her case. Although the testimony is taken under oath, and witnesses are subject to cross-examination, the proceedings are far less formal than those of a courtroom. The process of claiming a fair hearing is simple and informal; usually, a letter to the Medicaid caseworker who handled the application will suffice. However, there are strict time deadlines for doing so. Unfortunately, in New Hampshire it can take many months to get a decision from the hearings examiner after the hearing is conducted. One of the authors was involved in a fair hearing in October 2004, and, as of July 2005, has yet to receive a decision.

It is important to note that, under federal law, a nursing home cannot discriminate, discharge or in any way alter the treatment of a Medicaid patient. If, shortly before a private pay patient switches to Medicaid, the facility transfers the patient to a hospital or to another part of the facility, you have cause to investigate and determine whether the move was medically justified. Additionally, any facility that accepts federal funds, such as Medicare or Medicaid, has no legal right to require that other family members contribute to the payment or guarantee payment. Any contracts providing such guarantees are void.

Recently, New Hampshire has become much more aggressive in auditing closed Medicaid files. That is, after an application has been approved and the patient been on Medicaid, the state has the right to re-open the file for the purpose of making sure that the application has been handled correctly. On these audits, it is not unusual for the state to request more information or documentation from the applicant. At the initial interview, the case technician explains to each applicant that the state has the right of audit, so that everyone knows an audit is possible. In practice, though, going through such an audit can be a nerve-wracking experience. In many cases, the information request is sent to the nursing home patient's elderly spouse, who doesn't really understand what is going, on, and starts to worry if the other spouse will be taken off the Medicaid rolls. Or, the request is sent to the patient's adult child, who now has to take time from his or her schedule to go through old records on what they thought was a closed issue. They also start to worry that Mom or Dad will lose Medicaid. Again, this is a taste of the new reality of Medicaid in New Hampshire.

b. *Medicaid's Financial Requirements*
1. *General Rules*
Medicaid law puts very strict limits on the amount and type of assets that a recipient is allowed to have. Certain

types of assets are not counted towards eligibility and, accordingly, are called "non-countable assets," whereas certain assets are countable.   You are allowed to have unlimited non-countable assets, but there are limits on the countable assets you may have.   Non countable assets include, among others:

a. Your home. Your principal residence is not countable, regardless of value. Note that only one residence is exempt, so that if you have a vacation home, investment property or second home, the non homestead property will be countable.

b. Prepaid funeral contracts, as long as they are irrevocable, i.e, as long as you do not have the right to cancel the contract for a refund. Some states have limits on the amount that can be paid for the funeral. Note that the payment must be for the cost of the funeral. That is, you cannot "overpay," for the funeral, and then get a refund of any unused amounts after the funeral.

c. One burial plot for the applicant and spouse.

d. Essential household items, such as appliances, clothing, household furnishings and personal, non-investment jewelry.

e. Property subject to legal proceedings, such as property in probate.

    f. Lump sum death benefits for funeral and burial expenses.

    g. Income tax refunds.

    h. One motor vehicle. Some states put a cap on the value of the vehicle.

    i. Cash value of life insurance policies, up to $1,500. Insurance is only exempt if the face value is below $1,500. If the face value exceeds $1,500, then the cash value is added up, and only $1,500 is exempt.

    j. Term life insurance, with no cash value.

    k. Cash assets up to $2,000 or $2,500, depending on the state.

All other assets are countable, with no exceptions. Examples of countable assets are bank accounts, IRAs and similar retirement accounts, cash value of life insurance above $1,500, stocks, bonds and mutual funds, second homes, second cars, deferred annuities, and *anything* else of whatever kind or description that can be sold or turned into cash.

If you have countable assets over the allowable limit, you will not be eligible for Medicaid until you have spent down to the limit. This process is known as the "spend-down" and is discussed later. Alternatively, and the very point of this book, is that there are certain very powerful

Medicaid planning devices you can use to preserve most, not all, of your countable assets and still allow you to qualify for Medicaid.

Medicaid has separate rules for income. In the case of a single person, all of the income, with certain exceptions, must be paid to the nursing home. You are allowed to keep a minimal "personal needs allowance" of $50 per month as well as sufficient money to pay for health insurance premiums. In the case of a married couple, the income of the healthy spouse is not counted, while the income of the institutionalized spouse is. The healthy spouse does have the benefit of certain income protections, discussed below.

2. *Division of Assets for Married Couples*

Under a law ironically known as the "Spousal Impoverishment" provisions of the Medicare Catastrophic Coverage Act of 1988, the healthy spouse benefits from certain, albeit minimal, asset protections. Unfortunately, these protections can hardly be called protections at all. In Medicaid parlance, the nursing home spouse is known as the "Institutionalized Spouse," and the spouse living at home is known as the "Community Spouse." Congress, in passing the Spousal Impoverishment law, recognized that it would not be in society's interest to completely impoverish the community spouse. Under the Spousal Impoverishment law, the community spouse is entitled to keep half of the couple's countable assets, up to a maximum of about $95,000.

It makes no difference whose name the assets are in, and it makes no difference who brought the asset to the marriage. Many spouses, especially those involved in second marriages, take false comfort from the fact that they hold their assets in separate names or from the fact that they have entered into a premarital agreement. When a spouse in a second marriage enters a nursing home, however, the community spouse is in for an extremely uncomfortable surprise: whose name the asset is in, or whether there is a premarital agreement, is *completely irrelevant.* When a couple says, "I do," they are, for Medicaid purposes, consenting to treat their assets as if they were jointly held – in the eyes of the law, the marital unit has one pocketbook. The very most that the community spouse can keep is half, but no more than the maximum of $95,000.

The "protection" provided by the Spousal Impoverishment law is not automatic — it must be requested by the community spouse. The procedure by which the Community Spouse requests this asset protection is known as a "Resource Assessment." Once the institutionalized spouse enters a hospital or skilled or intermediate nursing facility and is likely to remain institutionalized for 30 consecutive days or more, the community spouse is entitled to have the resource assessment done. The resource assessment does not have to be done at that time, and it can be done later, as part of the Medicaid application itself, after the spend-down has taken place. However, the community spouse would be well advised to do the resource assessment as early as possible. As the resource assessment is essentially a financial "snapshot" of the assets on the date of institutionalization, it is easier to get the needed financial records shortly after the fact than months or, sometimes, years later. The documentation required to process a resource assessment is the same as that needed for a full application.

The mechanics of a resource assessment are as follows. All countable assets are added, and the total is divided by two. The result is called the "spousal share." For couples with assets of up to approximately $38,000, the community spouse may keep a total of about $19,000 even if that amount is higher than half of the total. For those couples with assets above $40,000, the community spouse may keep half, up to a cap of approximately $95,000.

3. *Treatment of Income for Married Couples*

How does Medicaid treat income? Once the asset tests have been met, the state will then consider the income of the married couple. Subject to deductions for the personal needs allowance and medical insurance, the income of the institutionalized spouse must be paid to the nursing home, in full. However, depending on the couple's circumstances, the community spouse may be allowed to keep some of the income of the institutionalized spouse, instead of this income being paid to the nursing home. Under federal law, each state must establish a "Minimum Monthly Maintenance Needs Allowance (MMNA)." The MMNA must be at least 150% of the federal poverty line for a family of two, and it rises each January 1. The MMNA currently ranges from a low of $1,604 to a high of $2,377.

If the community spouse's income is below the MMNA, he will be entitled to an "allowance" from the income of the institutionalized spouse. There is formula set by the federal government to establish the spousal income allowance. There are two ways, using Medicaid planning techniques, of raising the community spouse's monthly income allowance. First, the community spouse can request a fair hearing, claiming financial distress. Alternatively, he or she can seek a court order of support against the institutionalized spouse. If the court finds that the community spouse is entitled to higher income, then the court order would supersede the amount that the state Medicaid agency determined by the process explained above.

4. *The Spend-Down*

Due to Medicaid's strict asset limits, many people need to spend down their assets in order to qualify for benefits. If you need to do this, there are certain send down strategies that can help you. As mentioned above, certain assets are not countable for Medicaid purposes. It is perfectly permissible to spend money on non-countable assets, as long as you pay fair value for them. For example, a prepaid funeral contract is not a countable asset. In this way, the funeral is paid for out of the spend-down funds, *i.e.*, the funds that would otherwise have gone to the nursing home, and not the funds protected for the community spouse. One car per family is also not countable. Therefore, the community spouse can trade in the old car and buy a new one. He or she can also buy furniture, personal items, home improvements and repairs, all without limit, or pay down bills. Care should be taken, however, not to buy items such as expensive jewelry, artwork, or a luxury car, as these items may be considered to be investments, which would then be countable.

Whether assets are liquidated by making purchases or by paying the nursing home (obviously the last resort), attention must be given to the tax consequences of the spend-down. Many people today hold the bulk of their wealth in retirement assets such as IRAs and 401(k)s. There are significant income tax consequences when these assets are liquidated. The same is true of appreciated assets such as stocks and real estate and assets with a taxable component, such as savings bonds and annuities. In planning the spend-down, you need to be sensitive to the income tax consequences of liquidating assets. Therefore, it is very often advisable to consult with an accountant or financial advisor prior to finalizing plans as to the order in which assets should be liquidated.

Spending down in accordance with the state requirements, however, can be viewed as a last resort. We have already seen some modest techniques that can minimize what the patient and spouse have to spend. The field of Medicaid planning, which we discuss in later chapters, can actually allow you to save the bulk of your wealth while making you eligible for Medicaid.

Chapter 4:

Medicaid Planning For Those in a Nursing Home or About to Go into One

A. The Ethics of Medicaid Planning

Our first book, *Alzheimer's Disease: Fighting for Financial Survival*, defined Medicaid planning as structuring your assets in a way that protects them from being depleted by the nursing home, while making yourself eligible for Medicaid benefits. In the past few years a debate has raged in New Hampshire editorial pages and in the legislature as to the ethics of Medicaid planning. The argument against Medicaid planning is that it artificially makes people eligible for public benefits that were designed for the poor. United States Secretary of Health and Human Services Mike Leavitt said in a February 2005 speech:

> Medicaid must not become an inheritance protection plan. Right now, many older Americans take advantage of Medicaid loopholes to become eligible for Medicaid by giving away assets to their children. There is a whole industry that actually helps people shift costs to the taxpayer. There are ways families can preserve assets without shifting the costs of long-term care to Medicaid. We must close these loopholes and focus Medicaid's resources on helping

those who really need it. Doing so will save $4.5 billion during the next decade.

—*Speech to World Health Care Congress, Marriott Wardman Park Hotel, Washington, D.C., February 1, 2005.*

This and similar arguments have been made with increasing fervor in view of the federal and state budget crises of recent years.

We take the opposite view and believe that Medicaid planning is legal, moral and ethical, for the following reasons:

1. *Most Medicaid Planning is for the Benefit of the Spouse, not the Children.*

As we saw from an earlier chapter, the Medicaid law offers little by the way of protection for the healthy spouse. The healthy spouse is allowed to keep the home, plus half of the assets up to a cap of approximately $95,000. At first blush, this does not look so bad. A closer look, however, will reveal just how harsh and punitive it is. Remember, the healthy spouse only gets half the assets or $95,000, *whichever is less*. So, for example, if the monetary assets are $120,000, then the healthy spouse can keep only $60,000. If the assets are $100,000, then the healthy spouse can keep $50,000, and so on. This meager amount is all the savings the spouse has to live on for the rest of his or her life. With the cost of health care, gasoline, state and local taxes as well as other expenses out of sight, this paltry financial limit on the healthy spouse is a frightening thought indeed.

In our view, it is wrong to have the spouse of a

nursing home patient live a life of poverty or near poverty, especially after he or she has worked and saved a whole life to avoid living in poverty in old age. It is wrong for this spouse to worry about paying for a roof, furnace, or water heater when those things need to be replaced. It is shameful that the law puts the healthy spouse - more often than not elderly and living on a fixed income - in such a financial predicament. We invite Secretary Leavitt to sit down and have coffee with an elderly senior living in a triple decker on the West Side of Manchester, a senior who has spent most of her money because her husband is in the nursing home, and find out how she is forced to live. For her, the concept of the "Golden Years" is a cruel hoax, as most of the money she has spent a lifetime saving is gone. If there is any possibility that Secretary Leavitt has an open mind, he will very quickly realize that Medicaid planning is not about being an "inheritance protection plan" but is about helping elderly, vulnerable seniors with a spouse in the nursing home end out their years with some financial dignity.

We have also always been of the belief that the number of senior citizens who use Medicaid planning to shelter their assets is fairly insignificant. An important new study has borne this out. In May 2005, Georgetown University issued a report that said, in part:

> Research demonstrates that a large proportion of the disabled elderly in the community (who are at risk of nursing home placement) have limited assets. Many qualify for Medicaid in the

community, and most would qualify for Medicaid at admission to a nursing home. Most of the elderly with disabilities in the community have too little wealth to warrant hiring an attorney to arrange an asset transfer. Moreover, studies that look at who pays for nursing home care find that, even though they have limited resources, a large proportion of the elderly pay their own way throughout their nursing home stays, and that the elderly are less likely to rely on Medicaid than would be predicted given their resources.

There is little evidence that large numbers of the elderly are planning their estates for the purpose of gaining easy access to Medicaid in the event they need nursing home care. There is no evidence that they use transfers [of assets] or trusts to significantly shift the cost burdens to Medicaid, and little evidence that those who do transfer sizeable assets gain eligibility for Medicaid.

—Georgetown University Long-Term Care Financing Project, "Medicaid's Coverage of Nursing Home Costs: Asset Shelter for the Wealthy or Essential Safety Net," by Ellen O'Brien, May 2005, p. 3.

This study confirms what we, as experienced elder law professionals, have known for years, that most people do not use Medicaid planning to shelter their assets, and the study directly contradicts the unsupported statements to the contrary that Secretary Leavitt made in his February 2005 speech.

2. *The Law of Health Care Financing for the Elderly is Irrational and Unfair, and Medicaid Planning is a Response*

The current system of health care financing for the elderly is irrational and unfair. Consider the example of two people, both age 75. One person develops cancer, and his treatment will cost $300,000. Medicare and Medicare Supplement insurance will cover most of the cost, and financially, he will be in good shape. The other person in our example develops Alzheimer's Disease. He will go to the nursing home, and his care will likewise cost $300,000. However, neither Medicare nor Medicare Supplement will pay for any of his care. So, somewhere along the way society has made the decision that conditions requiring hospital or medical care will be covered, but chronic conditions requiring long-term nursing home care, such as Alzheimer's or Parkinson's, will not. There is absolutely no rational reason for society to cover one condition but not the other. Medicaid planning seeks to correct this imbalance and give some rationality to a broken system that does not make sense.

3. *There is Nothing Wrong with Leaving an Inheritance for the Children*

The vast majority of our clients are far from wealthy. They are ordinary citizens who have worked in the trades, in factories or in mom-and-pop type small businesses. By hard work, ingenuity and frugal living, they have paid for a house, educated their children and built up a modest nest egg. For the most part, today's seniors are decent, moral people who have saved, lived modestly, and paid their taxes without complaint over a lifetime. They are the people who have laid the foundation of the success that our society now enjoys.

Most of these people earnestly want to leave a small legacy to their children and grandchildren. Contrary to the opponents of Medicaid planning, who try to instill guilt over leaving an inheritance, we think that doing so is an honorable thing and is the right of every citizen. Let us be clear: We are not talking of leaving vast fortunes or beachfront mansions to the children at taxpayer expense. That is a different issue entirely. We are talking, rather, about passing down a modest house that someone has spent 30 years paying for, or a relatively small bank account, or a CD that can help a struggling family pay for college tuition. These people could very easily have spent the money during their lives, but have chosen not to do so and to live modestly so that they could help their children. No opponent of Medicaid planning has ever been able to adequately explain why this is a bad thing. We believe that everyone has the right to help and protect their spouse, children and grandchildren, and there is nothing unethical about doing so.

B. Different Types of Medicaid Planning

1. Asset Transfers

In the field of elder law, nothing is more misunderstood —or misused — than gifting assets. When used properly, gifting can shelter about half of the assets of someone who is in a nursing home or about to go into one. When used improperly, gifting can cause Medicaid disqualification, taxes, and loss of assets.

Central to gifting is an understanding of the transfer of asset rules. Essentially, the transfer of asset rules state that if a gift is made within three (or sometimes five) years of applying for Medicaid, then the donor (maker) of the gift will be disqualified for Medicaid benefits. The length of the disqualification will increase with the size of the gift. More precisely, the length of the disqualification will be equal to the size of the gift divided by the average private-pay nursing home rate in the state (the "disqualification rate"). The idea is that, if you gave away sufficient assets to pay for, say, six months in the nursing home, then you will be unable to qualify for Medicaid benefits for six months. If you give away sufficient assets to pay for one year, you will be disqualified for one year, and so on. Currently in New Hampshire, the disqualification rate is $6,004 per month.

The transfer-of-asset rule ties into another Medicaid concept, that of a "lookback period." There is a 36-month lookback period for transfers of assets to individuals, and a 60-month lookback period for transfers to irrevocable trusts. That is, Medicaid can only ask about, or look back on, transfers that have occurred within the past 36 months, or 60 months to an irrevocable trust. If you gave away a $100,000 asset to your son 37 months ago, Medicaid will not take the gift into account because the gift fell outside of the lookback period. However, if you gave a $100,000 asset to your son within the 36-month lookback period, then you will be disqualified from Medicaid for 16 months ($100,000 divided by $6,004). Theoretically, the potential period of Medicaid disqualification is unlimited. That is, if you gave away

$1,000,000 and apply for Medicaid within the 36-month lookback, you will be disqualified from Medicaid for 166 months, or nearly 14 years! If, on the other hand, you gave away $1,000,000 and apply for Medicaid 37 months later, the gift will have been outside of the lookback period, and your disqualification will be limited to 36 months. As you can see, failure to comply with these technical aspects of the law can be very costly, indeed.

There are certain exceptions to the transfer-of-asset rules that pertain to the family home. In these circumstances, a transfer of the home is not penalized:

> To avoid foreclosure;
> To a spouse or to a child who is blind or permanently or totally disabled;
> To an adult child who has lived in the house and provided care to the parent, such that the parent was kept out of the nursing home for two years;
> To a sibling who has an equity interest in the home, and who resided there for at least one year prior to the individual's admission to the nursing home.

Granite Care has tried to change these rules. Note that we said, "tried" to change the rules. Whether the change will ultimately be successful remains to be seen. That is, the Granite Care plan that passed the legislature changed the lookback period for gifts to individuals from three years to five but kept the lookback period for trusts the same as it is now, five years. Most significantly, under Granite Care, the disqualification period will start not when the gift is made as it is now, but when the Medicaid application is filed and the applicant, but for the gift, would otherwise be qualified for Medicaid. A simple example will illustrate: Under pre-Granite Care law, say someone makes a gift of $60,000 on August 1. Ten months later, on the following June 1, the disqualification caused by the gift will be over, and, all things being equal, the person will be Medicaid eligible. Under Granite Care, the start of the disqualification period will be delayed until the Medicaid application is filed at any time within five years of the gift. So say the person goes into the nursing home two years after making the gift. He or she is out of money and applies for Medicaid. The person will not be Medicaid eligible for another ten months after applying for Medicaid, since the disqualification period will not even have started until the application was filed.

This feature of Granite Care can be devastating to anyone who has made a gift within the past five years and who does not have enough money to pay for a nursing home. If someone has made a gift for *any purpose whatsoever*, including a gift to charity or church, a wedding gift to a grandchild, a gift of college tuition, or a gift to a child to help him out of a tough financial spot, for example, and if that person goes into a nursing home within the following five years and applies for Medicaid, he or she could be in some very big trouble: He could find himself disqualified for Medicaid for perhaps a very long time, all for having been good to someone by having made a gift. The person's intention in making the gift is completely irrelevant. Except for the very wealthy who can afford nursing homes, we believe that Granite Care will cause gifting to end in the State of New Hampshire.

Fortunately, this element of Granite Care is not in effect

yet and might never come into effect. The reason is that, in order for this feature of Granite Care to be implemented, the state has to ask for approval from the federal government. Such approval is known as a "Medicaid Waiver." In order for the state to request a Medicaid waiver, the governor needs to approve. At least as of this writing, the Governor's Office has indicated that the governor does not approve. The governor's opposition might put an end to this feature of Granite Care even before it leaves the starting gate.

Let's say that the current governor or some future governor perhaps, does approve, however. Then, the federal government would still need to approve. Three other states - Connecticut, Massachusetts and Minnesota - have filed requests for similar waivers. The oldest of these waiver requests has been pending about three years, and thus far, the federal government has not acted. In fact, Connecticut actually withdrew its waiver request in May 2005, noting that the request must be problematic if it has taken so long for the federal government to approve. A press release issued by Governor M. Jodi Rell's office stated:

> Although the waiver application was submitted in good faith, I continue to hear concerns from Connecticut residents about their future ability to access services at skilled nursing facilities if Medicaid eligibility processes are changed....
> As our frail elderly and disabled citizens attempt to navigate the complexity of the healthcare system, measures in the waiver application to change the process could be perceived as

hindering the ability of individuals to access appropriate nursing home care. In addition, while we are working to shore up the financial structure of our skilled nursing facilities, the waiver as crafted could lead to further deterioration of the already fragile financing of these facilities.

—Gov. M. Jodi Rell, Press Release, May 6, 2005.

Thus far, then, this punitive, anti-senior oriented feature of Granite Care has not been implemented, and hopefully will never be implemented. Since this feature of Granite Care is not in effect, let us look at the various methods of Medicaid Planning using asset transfers.

a. *Paying for Three (Or Five) Years and the Half-a-Loaf*
Two powerful Medicaid Planning devices are derived from the lookback and transfer of asset rules. Both of these devices work for people who are in a nursing home now or who are about to go into one. First, if you are fortunate enough to be able to pay privately for three years' worth of care, then you can gift all of your assets above that amount and use the remainder to pay for the care. (If Granite Care's change in lookback rules is enacted, then the three years discussed here would rise to five years.) Three years in a nursing home could easily be expected to cost between $250,000 and $300,000. Thus, one Medicaid planning technique would be to escrow enough money to cover the payments required within the 36-month lookback period. All assets above that level can be safely gifted away. As we will discuss shortly, however, it is very important to whom you make

the gift. You almost never want to gift the asset to your child, because the assets are then subject to your child's liabilities and life circumstances. For example, say your assets are $450,000. You keep $300,000 on hand to cover three years' worth of payments and gift your daughter the rest. She is married to someone whom you detest. Your daughter gets sick and passes away unexpectedly, and her will leaves all of your money to the evil son-in-law. He then remarries, and the money is gone. As you can see, gifting money to your spouse or children is fraught with difficulties and uncertainties, and the money just might not be available if you need to get it back.

Therefore, it is essential to have the recipient of the gift not hold the funds in his own name but place them into what is known as a "gift trust," or an irrevocable "creditor protection trust." Such a trust will not die and will not get divorced or remarried or be sued. It can be structured so as to be protected from creditors. The trust is like a protective wrapper around the money, safeguarding it from your children's creditors and whatever trouble they may get into.

Another very powerful technique involving gifting is the so-called "Half-a-Loaf" strategy. Under the half-a-loaf, it is possible to shelter approximately half of the assets, even if the person is *already in the nursing home*. That is, taking into account all of the assets, income, expenses and the state disqualification rate, it is possible to calculate the amount of money needed to cover the disqualification caused by a lump-sum gift. Factoring in all of these variables, it is generally possible, with a half-a-loaf, to shelter between 40 and 60 percent of the person's assets. To take a simple example, say the assets are $100,000. As we discussed previously, New Hampshire's disqualification rate is $6,004. A gift of $50,000 is made, which will disqualify the nursing home patient from benefits for eight months. The remaining $50,000 will, roughly speaking, be sufficient to cover the next eight months' worth of nursing home charges. At the end of the eight-month period, the applicant will be Medicaid eligible, and we have saved about half of the assets. It's more complex than presented in this simple example, of course, but, as can be seen, the half-a-loaf is a powerful tool that can protect a significant amount of assets.

As explained above, Granite Care has unsuccessfully tried to end half-a-loaf planning by delaying the start of the disqualification period until the Medicaid application is filed and the person is otherwise eligible for Medicaid. In order for the state to implement this drastic change, as discussed before, a federal waiver is necessary. Unless and until a waiver is granted, half-a-loaf planning can be done in the usual way.

Even if the waiver is granted, though, the half-a-loaf can still be done, though in a different way. The law states that any Medicaid disqualification is removed if the gifted assets are returned. Let's look at a simple example. Say that Grandmother is in the nursing home. Her life savings are $60,000. Instead of giving half of the money to Grandson, she gives him the entire $60,000 and then immediately applies for Medicaid. We know that Medicaid will be denied, since, under Granite Care, the disqualification starts to run when the application is filed. However, the filing of the application will start the penalty clock ticking. Then, Grandson gives Grandmother back half of the money she previously gifted to him. We know that any penalty is removed if money is returned. Therefore, the return of $30,000 will cut five months from the penalty. Grandmother uses this $30,000 (plus her Social Security) to pay for the next five months. When the five months is over, so is the penalty. We apply again for Medicaid, and this time it will be approved! So, even if the federal waiver is granted and Granite Care goes into effect, we will still be able to use half-a-loaf planning.

Frequently, half-a-loaf planning is done by one of the adult children acting as attorney in fact. If this is the case, then extreme care must be used in how the half-a-loaf is done. First, the power of attorney must be scrutinized to see if it contains provisions allowing the attorney in fact to make gifts. Assuming that it contains the correct language, the attorney in fact must make a good-faith determination that gifting is in the best interests of the Medicaid applicant, and that the applicant, had he or she been competent, would him or herself have authorized gifting. If these tests are met, then the proper type of trust must be designed to hold the gifted funds, and the terms of this trust should match, as closely as possible, the terms of the applicant's will.

Brief mention needs to be made of the Health Insurance Portability and Accountability Act of 1996. Section 217 of the Act stated that anyone who disposes of assets with the purpose of obtaining Medicaid assistance is guilty of a crime. Popularly referred to as the "Granny Goes to Jail law," the statute shortly came under heavy criticism from seniors' groups, legal scholars and the bar. The result was that the statute was amended so as to exonerate clients from criminal responsibility but to impose criminal penalties on paid advisors who counseled clients about the disposal of assets during the penalty period.

Fortunately, attorneys no longer have to worry about the criminal statute. In March 1998, Attorney General Janet Reno, in a letter to then Speaker of the House Newt Gingrich, advised that the Justice Department would not be enforcing the statute, due to serious questions about its constitutionality. At the same time, the New York State Bar Association sued the Justice Department, alleging that the law was unconstitutional. Ultimately, on September 14, 1998, the Federal District Court found that the law was unconstitutional on First Amendment grounds and entered a permanent injunction against the Justice Department from enforcing it. Therefore, the law, having been declared unconstitutional, and invalidated by the courts, is no longer a cause for concern. While it technically is on the books, no one pays any attention to it any more, and, in effect, it has become a nullity.

Before leaving the topic of gifting, an explanation of the tax consequences of gifting needs to be made. Most people know that you can gift $11,000 to anyone per year without any tax consequences. However, very few people understand the tax consequences of making gifts above this amount. Luckily, in most Medicaid planning cases, there will be absolutely no gift tax consequences. First, it is important to understand that there is no income tax whatsoever on a gift. Rather, the tax burden falls on the person who makes the gift. The donor, or maker, of a gift of above $11,000 to any person in any one year must report the gift to the IRS by April 15 of the following year, on a gift tax return, IRS Form 709. Fortunately, however, each citizen has a lifetime gifting limit, tax free, of $1,000,000. Since the vast majority of people who do nursing home planning have far less than this amount, it is almost always the case that no taxes will be due.

2. Annuities

a. Immediate Auunities

Another very powerful type of Medicaid planning technique involves the use of a certain type of annuity known as an "immediate annuity." An immediate annuity is a financial transaction in which you transfer a sum of money, usually to an insurance company, in exchange for monthly payments of principal and interest back to you. Think about a promissory note. With a promissory note, you transfer a sum of money to a borrower. In exchange, the borrower pays you back in monthly installments of principal and interest. The biggest difference between a promissory note and an immediate annuity, however, concerns the length of the payment term. With a promissory note, the payments can be for any length of time agreed to by lender and borrower. With an immediate annuity, however, the length of payments is based on the "lender's" life expectancy. In the case of a married couple, an immediate annuity can shelter money, *sometimes as much as 100%*, from long-term care. This is the result of two different laws pertaining to spend-down in the case of a married couple. Recall from our discussion of the spend-down rules that the community spouse is permitted to keep half of the monetary assets, up to a cap of about $95,000. If a married couple has $150,000, the healthy spouse can keep $75,000, and the rest (except for $2,500) would have to be spent down. Significantly, the law says that the spend-down funds do not have to be spent on the nursing home! Those funds can be spent for any purpose, as long as fair value is received and as long as they are spent for the benefit of either spouse. The other relevant law concerns income. The income of the community spouse is completely exempt from the nursing home bills of the sick spouse. So, if one spouse is in the nursing home on Medicaid, and the other spouse has a job or otherwise gets income, then such income does not need to be used for the sick spouse's nursing home bill.

The key to annuity planning, then, is to re-structure the finances to convert assets, which are fully countable for the nursing home, to income for the healthy spouse, which is completely exempt. In the above example with a $75,000 spend-down, the healthy spouse uses the spend-down money to buy an immediate annuity. The annuity is structured so that the payments go to the healthy spouse. In this way, the sick one immediately qualifies for Medicaid, the monthly annuity payments go to the healthy one, and all of the spend-down money has been preserved. The risk in this case is that the healthy spouse would him or herself later need to go into a nursing home during the life of the annuity. In this event, the annuity payments will have to be spent on his or her care.

While immediate annuities work well for married

couples, the State of New Hampshire has effectively put a stop to their use for single people. As a result of a law change in August 2003, the State of New Hampshire has to be the beneficiary of the annuity of an unmarried person. In other words, any money left in the annuity contract at the nursing home resident's death would need to go to the State. Therefore, the use of annuities for unmarried people has essentially come to a halt. Fortunately, however, the new law does <u>not</u> pertain to the healthy spouse buying an annuity. Therefore, as to married people, the annuity is still a valuable planning tool.

There are two types of immediate annuities, commercial annuities and private annuities. A commercial annuity is done through an insurance company. The advantage of a commercial annuity is that once it is done, there is nothing further to think about. All you need to do is to collect the check every month. The disadvantage of a commercial annuity is in the interest rate. The way the insurance company makes a profit is to invest the money at a higher rate of interest than is paid to you.

The second kind of immediate annuity is known as a private annuity. With a private annuity, an individual, usually one of your children, takes the place of the insurance company. That is, you transfer the money to a child, and he makes the monthly payments to you. The advantage of a private annuity is that the profit that the insurance company would have made with your money is, instead, kept in the family. The disadvantage of a private annuity is that you need to rely on your child or children to make the payments each month.

b. *Deferred Annuities*

One more word about annuities is in order. Generally, there are two types of annuities. One is the immediate annuity described above. If done correctly, as we have just seen, an immediate annuity will shelter large amounts of money from the nursing home. The other type of annuity is the deferred annuity. Many senior citizens use deferred annuities for investment purposes. In a deferred annuity, you deposit the money with the insurance company. Much like a bank CD, the insurance company pays interest on the principal of the annuity, and it grows in value. One major difference between a bank CD and an insurance company deferred annuity, however, is that a deferred annuity can be "annuitized," *i.e.*, surrendered to the insurance company, and converted to an immediate annuity of the type described above. Some unscrupulous insurance agents or investment advisors sell deferred annuities to senior citizens, with the false explanation that the annuity is "protected" from the nursing home, or that all the nursing home can get is the interest and not the principal. Such statements are outright deceptions.

A deferred annuity is a completely countable asset, offering no nursing home protection at all. The ability to quickly annuitize a deferred annuity, or convert it into an immediate annuity, is actually of little practical value, since virtually any monetary investment can be quickly sold and converted to an immediate annuity. Therefore, all seniors should be cautioned about the use of deferred annuities as Medicaid planning tools, since they have no use at all for this purpose.

Chapter 5:

Trusts and Medicaid Planning

Trusts are essential tools in Medicaid Planning. In this chapter, we will look at three different types of trusts that can be used to protect assets, the Irrevocable Medicaid Trust, the Pourover Trust and the Revocable Trust with Medicaid Triggers. All of these trusts are for people who have time to plan, i.e., people who are healthy now and want to protect themselves and their families should they become ill in the future.

A. The Irrevocable Medicaid Trust

For years, the Irrevocable Medicaid Trust has been the workhorse of Medicaid planning. With this trust, you receive all of the income and control the investments of the trust. Through the trust, you can buy and sell assets, including real estate such as the family home. On your death, the trust passes to the heirs without probate proceedings. During your lifetime, however, the trust is irrevocable and is subject to a five-year lookback period. The lookback concept is the same as that described earlier, when we spoke about gifting. That is, the value of the assets transferred to the trust is divided by the disqualification rate of $6,004 to determine the waiting period for the trust to shelter assets. For example, if your house is worth $300,000, the waiting period would be 50 months. If Granite Care is to go into effect, then the lookback would still be 60 months, but the monthly accrual of protection would be lost. That is, you would have to wait the full 60 months for the trust to become protected. Recall, however, that this feature of Granite Care requires a federal waiver to go into effect.

The disadvantage of the Medicaid trust is that you do not have direct access to the principal of the trust. The rule is simple – if you can get the money, the nursing home can get the money. If you can't get it, the nursing home can't get it. How then can you have access to the funds in the trust? The answer lies in a legal concept known as a "Special Power of Appointment." A special power of appointment is the ability to direct where assets are distributed. Here is how use the special power of appointment to obtain principal from the trust. Say you set up a Medicaid trust. You are the trustee, and you name your three children as beneficiaries. Now say that you want to obtain principal from the trust. (Remember, you are entitled to the income, in any event.) You, as trustee, take the money you want, and distribute it as a gift to one or more of your children. Remember, you can gift them $11,000 each per year without any tax reporting. Your children then take the money and gift it back to you. How do you guarantee that your children will gift the money back? Therein lies the magic of the special power of appointment. Under the special power of appointment, you are allowed to change the beneficiaries of the trust. In effect, you can "disinherit" your children from the trust, so that they receive no money at your death, and you make sure that your children know it. Faced with the prospect of being disinherited, the children, of course, will return the money.

Everyone uses the Medicaid trust differently. Some people use it to protect their house only, while others use it to protect some of their liquid assets, such as stocks or CDs. The Medicaid trust is ideal to protect your house from long-term care. Say your house is worth $250,000. With the New Hampshire disqualification rate of $6,004 per month, the house will be protected in 42 months. Since a house is not liquid, like money, the children have no involvement at all. You are free to sell the house through the trust if you want to, and buy another one in the trust, and the new one will be protected, as well.

B. The Pourover Trust

The Medicaid trust has long reigned supreme as an asset protection tool. Yet, there is another type of trust that approaches asset protection in a completely different way, the pourover trust. The pourover trust is revolutionary in that it allows a married couple to shelter assets from the nursing home using a trust that is completely revocable, that can be amended at any time and that allows the married couple to have unfettered access to their money.

Let's look at the pourover trust in more detail. It makes clever use of what is known as a "testamentary trust" coupled with a will and revocable trust. The federal law which underlies Medicaid is known as OBRA '93. Under OBRA '93, if a testamentary trust is written in the correct way, and the beneficiary of that trust enters a nursing home and applies for Medicaid, the principal of the testamentary trust will not be available to the nursing home; *i.e.*, it will be sheltered.

In the case of a married couple, in all but the most unusual case, one spouse will die before the other. Since we do not know who will be the first to die, we create a joint husband and wife revocable trust. The assets to be protected from the nursing home are placed into that trust. While both spouses are alive, they can use the trust assets as they wish, without any restrictions or involvement of the children. The trust states that on the first death, some or all of the assets are to "pour over" to the estate of the spouse who has died. At this point, the will of that spouse takes over. The will creates a testamentary trust for the benefit of the surviving spouse. That testamentary trust says that the funds are to be used for the care, comfort and maintenance of the surviving spouse, to maintain the spouse in his or her accustomed standard of living. Usually, one or more of the children act as trustees. Since testamentary trusts are exempt from the nursing home, the assets in the trust are protected! The nursing home does not have access to those assets.

In order to give the surviving spouse as much control over the trust as possible, the trust gives the spouse a special power of appointment and the right to gift trust principal to the beneficiaries. Just as in the Medicaid trust, the spouse can direct that assets be given to one or more of the children, and those children can then return those assets to the spouse.

The beauty of the pourover trust lies in the fact that

during the lifetime of both spouses, the trust is revocable, and the spouses are free to do whatever they want with the assets, without the children being involved at all. Additionally, the pourover trust, being revocable, has no lookback period. It is effective immediately, and it is also exempt from Granite Care. That is, even if Granite Care is fully implemented, the pourover trust will be unaffected. The trust can also be tailored to fit the needs of the client. That is, there is no requirement that all of the assets be placed into the trust. Whatever the couple wants to protect from the nursing home is put in the pourover trust, and the rest of the assets can be left out. It is our prediction that the pourover trust will become used more and more often as a Medicaid planning tool.

C. The Revocable Trust with Medicaid Triggers

Despite the fact that the Medicaid trust has a proven track record of protecting assets, it is not for everyone. Some people do not want to do anything having the label "irrevocable." Others do not want their children to have any involvement with their affairs. For these persons, there is an alternative. One of the predominant Medicaid planning tools has become, in recent years, the "Revocable Trust with Medicaid Triggers." The beauty of the revocable trust with Medicaid triggers is that it can allow your family to implement Medicaid planning for you in the future, if, due to illness or incapacity, you are no longer able to do so on your own. As we saw in an earlier chapter, a revocable trust is a legal document that serves the same purpose as a will, but which avoids probate at death. However, the revocable trust goes beyond mere probate avoidance, in that it also has provisions for a successor trustee, usually one of the children, to manage the trust in the event you become incompetent.

"Medicaid triggers," simply stated, are those things that your trustee or attorney in fact can do for you to protect assets. The more important of these things have been discussed in earlier chapters. Medicaid triggers are detailed provisions that specifically allow your trustee to do the following things, among others:

A. Represent you before the state Medicaid authorities, both in applying for benefits and in claiming a fair hearing;
B. Apply for a Resource Assessment;
C. Secure the Minimum Monthly Maintenance Needs Allowance;
D. Convert countable assets into non-countable ones;
E. Employ the caretaker child exception;
F. Rent your house, to make the house non-countable;
G. Do a Half-a-Loaf;
H. Enter into a commercial or private annuity;
I. Enter into a Life Care Contract;
J. Enter into a Self-Canceling Installment Note; and
K. Use whatever other techniques Congress may create in the future.

When you create a revocable trust with Medicaid triggers, it is also essential that you insert the triggers into the durable power of attorney that is usually done with the trust. The reason is that there are certain assets, such as IRAs, 401(k)s and other tax-deferred retirement accounts, that cannot be put into the name of the trust. Additionally, you may have forgotten to put all of your other assets into the trust name. Therefore, the successor trustee of the trust does not have the ability to do any Medicaid planning with these assets, since they are not a part of the trust. If, however, the durable power of attorney contains the triggers, then the attorney in fact would be able to shelter these assets as well.

Every revocable trust should have Medicaid triggers, even if the grantor of the trust (*i.e.*, the person who sets it up) is not concerned about nursing homes. Adding the triggers to a trust has no disadvantage whatsoever; rather, the triggers "set the stage," so to speak, for your successor trustee to engage in

Medicaid planning should the need arise later on.

Chapter 6:

The Social Security Tax Trap

In 1993, a modification to Social Security benefit taxation caused one of the largest tax increases to affect seniors in the history of our country. Very few seniors understood the significance of this change, and even fewer are taking advantage of planning techniques to reduce or eliminate this increase.

Before 1993, seniors paid taxes on half of their Social Security benefits if their combined income was $25,000 for individuals or $32,000 for married couples. In 1993, the portion of taxable Social Security increased to 85 percent, and individuals with "provisional" incomes above $34,000 and married couples with "provisional" incomes above $44,000 were subject to the higher rate of taxation. Those with provisional incomes below $25,000 and married couples with provisional incomes below $32,000 pay no taxes on their Social Security benefits.

Simply explained, provisional income is the sum of a person's wages if still employed, interest on his money, dividends from his investments, the net of capital gains/losses, any pension income (exclusive of Social Security), and any annuity or IRA distributions.

To this total, add one-half of the person's annual Social Security benefit, and if the sum of these is greater than $34,000 for a single taxpayer or $44,000 for a married couple, you fail the provisional income test, and your Social Security benefit is now taxed at the 85% threshold.

This increase has caused many seniors to pay much more in taxes over the last decade. Many have done nothing to counter the increase; they just pay more federal income tax.

Avoid the Mistake. Review your most recent tax return. Specifically, review line 8a (interest). For many seniors this number is large because of the large stockpiles of cash in savings accounts, certificates of deposit, or treasuries. The interest this money produces in the bank or in government bonds may be causing you to "fail" the provisional income test. The interest being generated on these accounts may be the cause of the 85% Social Security threshold!

Consider a shift to tax-efficient or tax-deferred investments to reduce line 8a or 9b on the tax return to a level where you would "pass" the provisional income test and enjoy the Social Security benefit without counting it as a taxable event. This is what you expected when you entered the system in the first place.

There are several techniques to properly eliminate or reduce the implications of this tax problem.

Using a tax-deferred annuity to solve the problem is but one method. In addition to an annuity, shifting assets to "tax- efficient" planning also works well to reduce the exposure to the added tax.

Here is an example of a client couple that is currently "failing" the provisional income test:

Mr. and Mrs. John Client have been enjoying their retirement years. Their total household income is $55,000, and they have an adjusted gross income of $52,000. Not all Social Security benefits are taxable, as shown below.

Wages	$ 0
Interest (line 8a)	$ 20,000
Pension	$ 15,000
Social Security (line 20a)	$ 20,000

Determining how much of Social Security is taxable is a two-part process as described earlier.

First, determine the household income exclusive of Social Security benefits paid.

Interest (line 8a)	$ 20,000
Pension	$ 15,000
Household income	$ 35,000

Second, add the household income and one-half the annual Social Security benefit.

Household income	$ 35,000
One-half annual Social Security benefit	$ 10,000
Total	$ 45,000

$45,000 is greater than the top of the provisional income threshold of $44,000. As a result, this couple is taxed on 85 percent of their $20,000 Social Security benefit, increasing their taxable earnings by $6,850

How to Return Social Security Back to Tax-free Status. Mr. and Mrs. Client decide to shift most of their bank cash (which they don't plan to use but like to keep safe) into a fixed annuity. The interest is not taxable unless withdrawn. The results:

Wages	$ 0
Interest (line 8a)	$ 3,000 [1]
Pension	$ 15,000
Social Security	$ 20,000

First, determine the household income exclusive of Social Security benefits paid. Next, add one-half of the annual Social Security benefit.

Household income	$ 18,000
One-half Social Security benefit	$ 10,000
Total	$ 28,000

This $28,000 is less than the bottom provisional income test of $32,000. As a result, the clients are taxed on none of their Social Security benefit. This decreases their taxable earnings by nearly $7,000 accomplished simply by shifting the manner in which they allocate their savings.

Many seniors make the mistake to focus on estate taxes and forget about using techniques that prevent the confiscation of wealth via the income tax. The income tax consequences of your actions or inactions can make a world of difference for you and your family. Spend some time reviewing your tax returns, and consider seeking advice to determine what planning opportunities would be best suited for your goals and objectives.

---

[1] Client maintains over $50,000 in bank for emergencies or opportunities."

Chapter 7:

Net Unrealized Appreciation

Many retirees have accumulated very large 401(k) balances or other qualified plans as a result of a career's worth of savings. For some, a large percentage of your plan consists of highly appreciated individual company stock. The tax savings you can generate using the NUA (net unrealized appreciation) technique can make a significant impact on your financial and estate planning.

Unfortunately, many retirees and many advisors make a fundamental mistake: they roll the qualified plan rich in employer stock to an IRA. Often retirees and advisors assume rolling to an IRA is the only option available. On the surface this seems like the standard operating procedure, but if this option is exercised you may cost your family thousands of dollars in additional taxes they should not have to pay!

A. NUA Explained

NUA occurs when an employer-sponsored plan allows the employee to purchase employer securities as part of the qualified retirement plan. The Internal Revenue Service treats these securities held inside the plan differently than it treats other assets such as cash and mutual funds when an employee retires. When the employee rolls over his qualified plan to an IRA, he has the opportunity to withdraw his employer securities and pay income tax on the cost basis (not the current value) and capital gains tax on the gain if he sells the employer securities. The cash, mutual funds, or other investment accounts will roll over to the IRA and are not taxed until withdrawn. (See IRS publication 575.)

Case Study

Mr. Smith, age 65, has a 401(k) plan valued at $500,000. $250,000 is mutual funds and $250,000 is company stock. The basis on the company stock is $50,000. Assume Mr. Smith is in the 25% federal income tax bracket.

Option 1: Normal rollover approach

Mr. Smith rolls the entire account to an IRA. Any normal distributions he takes will be taxed in the 25% federal income tax bracket. At age 70½, he will be forced to take required minimum distributions (RMD) and pay taxes on these distributions in his then applicable (assumed 25%) tax bracket. (See IRS Publication 590.)

Option 2: NUA rollover approach

Mr. Smith rolls the stock out of the 401(k) plan. The basis on the stock is $50,000, and he must pay ordinary income tax on the basis of $12,500 ($50,000 x 25% tax rate). The stock is transferred to a non-qualified account.

No additional taxes are owed on the stock until Mr. Smith sells it. Assume he does sell the stock. He pays capital gain tax on the sale vs. ordinary income and is thus taxed at 15% (current maximum capital gain tax rate), not 25%. This creates an immediate tax savings of 10%. Shares sold under this technique are taxed at long-term capital gain tax rates (up to the NUA) regardless of the length of time between the roll-out and the sale of the stock and short- or long-term gains on any additional gain beyond the NUA based on the time of sale. If he does not sell the stock, there are no additional taxes beyond the ordinary income tax due on the rollout. All other remaining funds are rolled to an IRA.

B. Benefits of NUA

First, by utilizing the NUA approach you will reduce your overall tax burden on the 401(k) plan and have the opportunity to use capital gain tax rates vs. ordinary income tax on $200,000 of the value of the account.

Second, by reducing the amount rolling into the IRA you will reduce the required distribution amounts when you reach age 70½. Required minimum distributions are calculated on the year end balance of the IRA, and if you remove the value of the stock from the account it will not be included in the RMD calculation.

Third, capital gain tax rates are significantly lower than the current income tax rates.

These tax savings can be used to fund long-term care and other estate preservation strategies using funds that otherwise would have been lost to taxes!

C. Drawbacks

This technique is designed primarily for those above age 59½. The early distribution penalties apply to those who elect this option under age 59½, and a 10% early distribution penalty will apply. The technique, however, may still be a viable option under these circumstances, as the penalty tax only pertains to the "basis" of the roll-out and not the full value of the stock.

NUA does not enjoy a "stepped-up basis" at death. When reviewing your overall estate planning objectives you must be aware that, unlike other highly appreciated securities you may own, the NUA stock will not receive the increase to market value at death and may present a large capital gain tax to the beneficiary. A plan to liquidate out of the NUA stock may be necessary to prevent erosion due to the tax the beneficiary will pay.

If you were an active trader within the qualified plan, buying and selling the employer stock, the basis may be significantly affected. If the market value of the stock is close to the basis of the stock, the benefits of using the NUA approach will be minimal. Under these circumstances, most of the roll-out would be taxed as ordinary income.

If you were not an active trader within your qualified plan, a thorough review of this planning technique may protect you and your family from yet another major tax trap!

Chapter 8:

The "Stretch" IRA

The single largest asset for many retirees other than their primary residence is their Individual Retirement Account ("IRA"), and most are completely unaware of the tax nightmare that awaits the beneficiaries of these accounts if the account holders have not properly established a plan to pass this tax-deferred asset to their spouses and children.

In 2001, the Internal Revenue Service overhauled the rules pertaining to mandatory distributions from IRA accounts, and as a result some excellent planning opportunities are now available. Today, with proper planning, your IRA accounts can live on for your family long after you are gone.

After an IRA owner's death, a spouse can roll the IRA into his/her name. This "spousal" rollover approach is widely known as a preferred planning technique to protect the spouse. Where most IRA planning goes awry is when the spouse dies and the children plan to inherit the asset. If the surviving spouse names a "designated" beneficiary of the IRA account, the beneficiary can withdraw the funds from the IRA over his or her life expectancy after the parent dies. The planning potential of this technique is tremendous. Under the old rules, the beneficiary would simply cash out the parent's IRA account and pay the income taxes on the distribution, resulting in massive taxes for most beneficiaries. With the new rules, the beneficiaries have a planning opportunity to take simply the RMD (Required Minimum Distribution) based on their life expectancy, and the remaining account balance can continue to grow on a tax-deferred basis. This technique is known as the "Stretch IRA." The beneficiary can elect to remove more than the required distribution at any time if he needs additional funds.

Case Study

Mr. John Smith, age 65, has an IRA valued at $100,000. Let's assume that he earns 6% on this IRA and will be taking only his Required Minimum Distributions once he is age 70½. Assume he has one child whom he names beneficiary of his IRA. His child (Bill) is age 40. Mr. Smith's required distribution schedule will look like this:

Mr. John Smith's IRA
Assuming 6% Return on Investment and Taking Only RMDs

Year	Age	Required Distribution ($)	Account Value 12/31($)
2005	65	0	106,000
2006	66	0	112,360
2007	67	0	119,102
2008	68	0	126,248
2009	69	0	133,823
2010	70	4,884	136,968
2011	71	5,169	140,017
2012	72	5,469	142,949
2013	73	5,787	145,738
2014	74	6,123	148,359
2015	75	6,479	150,782
2016	76	6,854	152,976
2017	77	7,216	154,938
2018	78	7,632	156,602
2019	79	8,031	157,967
2020	80	8,447	158,998
2021	81	8,883	159,655
2022	82	9,337	159,898
2023	83	9,810	159,682
2024	84	10,302	158,961
2025	85	10,741	157,758

Now let's assume Mr. Smith lives until age 85. When he dies, his son is age 61. His son has two choices.

First, he can simply cash out Dad's IRA (no stretch) and pay the income taxes due.

Lump Sum Account Liquidation in 2026	
Total distributions	$157,758
Federal income tax on	
total distribution	$ 41,230
Net after-tax to Bill	$116,528

Over 26% lost to taxes.

Second, Bill stretches the IRA.

Required Distributions from 2026 through 2050

Total distributions	$367,647
Federal income taxes	$ 60,735
Net after-tax income	$306,912

Only 16.5% lost to taxes.

With no stretch planning Bill will inherit $116,528, but with the stretch IRA planning he will inherit $306,912. With proper planning the IRA account will become a family heirloom and a multigenerational asset transferring event. (*The above calculation assumes son is married filing joint return and has taxable income of $50,000 excluding the required distributions.*)

How the Stretch Technique Works

Bill must begin taking required distributions from his father's IRA based on his own life expectancy starting the year following his father's death. His father's IRA is now worth $160,758, and his son, now age 61, must take a minimum distribution of $6,465.

Mr. Bill Smith's Inherited IRA
Assuming 6% Return on Investment and Taking Only RMDs

Year	Age	Required Distribution ($)	Account Value 12/31($)
2026	61	6,465	160,758
2027	62	6,870	163,534
2028	63	7,301	166,045
2029	64	7,759	168,249

2030	65	8,247	170,096
2031	66	8,768	171,534
2032	67	9,322	172,503
2033	68	9,914	172,940
2034	69	10,545	172,771
2035	70	11,219	171,918
2036	71	11,939	170,295
2037	72	12,709	167,804
2038	73	13,533	164,339
2039	74	14,416	159,784
2040	75	15,364	154,007
2041	76	16,384	146,864
2042	77	17,484	138,192
2043	78	18,675	127,809
2044	79	19,970	115,507
2045	80	21,390	101,047
2046	81	22,965	84,145
2047	82	24,749	64,445
2048	83	26,852	41,460
2049	84	29,614	14,333
2050	85	15,193	0

Bill must be listed as a "designated" beneficiary on the IRA beneficiary election form for the stretch option to be valid. The easiest way to understand a "designated beneficiary" is a beneficiary with a birth date. When the son notifies the custodian of the death of his father, he will most likely need to furnish a certified death certificate and also establish a beneficiary IRA account with the custodian. At that time the IRA provider will move the assets from the decedent's IRA into the "inherited" IRA account. Keep in mind the account will stay in the name of the deceased for the beneficiary's benefit but does not roll over into the son's IRA accounts.

Potential Pitfalls

If Mr. Smith failed to name a beneficiary or he named his estate as the beneficiary, his son would have only up to 5 years from the date of death to remove the value from the IRA account. This does not leave much planning opportunity.

If Mr. Smith names a trust as beneficiary, there are numerous potential negative consequences for his son. In most cases it is best to name the beneficiaries of the IRA accounts by name. The son will either use the 5-year rule to remove the IRA assets or, best case, he may be able to use the remaining life expectancy of Mr. Smith. Obviously Mr. Smith's life expectancy would be much shorter than his son's.

The current custodian who holds the IRA may not honor the stretch technique. This is a common but little understood problem with the IRA account. You should review the custodial agreement signed when you established your IRA account to see if the provider will allow the stretch. Surprisingly, not all custodians allow this to occur. The income tax ramifications of not stretching are severe. If your custodian does not honor the stretch you may want to consider moving your IRA account to a provider who does.

The power of the stretch IRA provides you with the opportunity to focus on multigenerational planning while maintaining 100% control of the account during your life.

Chapter 9:

IRA Tax Planning and the Power of the ROTH IRA

The largest transfer of wealth in the history of our country has begun. Many retirees have accumulated very large 401(k) balances or other qualified plans. For many the company retirement plan is the single largest asset other than their primary residence. Many retirees have planned properly for the disposition of their real estate but have neglected planning for the retirement account.

"The Jobs and Growth Tax Relief Reconciliation Act of 2003" has created wonderful planning opportunities for the informed senior. The tax code was enacted back in 1913, and with the tax package of 2003 we are enjoying the "luxury" of some of the lowest tax brackets in our country's history.

Current tax brackets (2005):

<u>10%</u>   Married couples earning less than $14,600 and single people earning less than $7,300 in taxable earnings are taxed in the 10% tax bracket.

<u>15%</u>   Married couples who earn less than $59,400 and

single people who earn less than $29,700 in taxable earnings are taxed in the 15% tax bracket.

25% Married couples who earn less than $119,950 and single people who earn less than $71,950 in taxable earnings are taxed in the 25% bracket.

Food for thought: Our government is allocating a huge amount of resources to fight the war on terrorism and the war in Iraq. Medicare is in a state of crisis. The Pension Benefit Guarantee Corporation (PBGC) is having solvency issues, and our nation's deficit and debt are reaching epic proportions while at the same time we are enjoying some of the lowest tax brackets since the tax code was adopted! Sooner or later our nation will have to change either its spending or our tax structure.

Retirees have been trained to avoid taking distributions from their IRA portfolios for two primary reasons. First, many are comfortably living on their Social Security benefits and pension incomes. Second, when retirees take money out of the retirement account they must do something they have been trained to avoid... pay income tax on the distribution. Many seniors delay the distribution event until it becomes mandatory at age 70$^{1}/_{2}$. (See publication 590.)

This is often a major financial planning mistake! One of the largest planning mistakes retirees make when it comes to the IRA account is waiting too long to begin the distribution process. Here's why. The IRA account is tax-deferred, not tax-free. When one spouse dies, the survivor is now forced to file a tax return as a "single taxpayer." Review the brackets for single people versus married couples. Married couples enjoy much wider 10% and 15% tax brackets versus single people. In fact, the brackets are cut in half! Many widows and widowers suddenly find themselves jumping into higher brackets and pay more income taxes when they become single taxpayers. Unfortunately, this is not a rare occurrence; it happens all too often. Finally, upon the survivor's death, the IRA is often taxed to the heirs at even higher tax brackets!

With some foresight, you can make the outcome much different.

First, review your tax return. Many seniors actually enjoy the 0% tax bracket, and most married couples are within the 10% or 15% tax bracket. The technique described next works best within these tax brackets. Taxes are eventually due on the IRA. The question is: should you prepay the tax now at the low brackets or delay?

Step 1: If you are already over 70$^1/_2$, take the MRD as required by law out of your IRA. If under age 70$^1/_2$, proceed directly to step 2.

Step 2: Using your previous year's tax return as a guide, run the math to determine what sources of income were reported and what the taxable income was. This is to be a guide. Please remember to consider any additional withdrawals you have taken from your IRA accounts, capital gains from the sale of any investments you hold, pension increases, and/or wages if you worked any part of the year.

Step 3: With this information, forecast what the taxable income will be for the current year.

Step 4: If you are "enjoying the luxury" of the 0%, 10% or 15% bracket, consider "converting" IRA assets to the Roth IRA to the extent that the you will remain within these low brackets. Caveat: you must review your Social Security benefits for inclusion into this calculation.

When you properly utilize this technique you will create a *tax-free* legacy. There will be no required distributions or additional taxes for the surviving spouse. When one spouse dies, a jump in brackets is less likely because there is no required distribution to pass through the single person's bracket. Even if there is not sufficient time to convert the entire IRA to the Roth, you have still reduced the IRA account value for the MRD calculation, resulting in a positive impact on your overall tax planning.

The Roth IRA provides a "one-two" punch by allowing you to reduce the pitfalls in the tax code for single taxpayers while creating a *tax-free* legacy for the family.

Chapter 10:

Final Thoughts

If the readers of this book are like most of our clients, they are senior citizens who have worked a lifetime building up a modest nest egg. They have worked hard, paid their mortgages, paid their taxes, provided for their families and have put money in the bank. Rather than complain or give up when life put obstacles in their path, they have kept on doing what they were taught as children: be diligent in their work and make the best of it.

This generation has been the most successful in history in saving and investing money, and, as this book has shown, there are two forces that can strip them of what they have saved over a lifetime and make it much harder to protect the family: the nursing home and the tax system. The nursing home is probably the single largest obstacle to legacy planning, yet most planners and most seniors do not plan for this contingency until it is too late. This lack of planning usually yields catastrophic financial results at the worst possible time.